THIS BOOK BELONGS TO:

_____

WELCOME TO MINNESOTA

Dedicated to all the explorers.

All rights reserved.
No part of this book may be reproduced in any form or by any means, electronic or mechanical, and no photocopying or recording, unless you have written permission from the author.

ISBN 978-1-958985-56-4

Text copyright © 2025 by Mimi Jones

www.joeysavestheday.com

A Mimi Book

Minnesota gets its name from the Dakota Sioux language. The word "Minnesota" comes from "Mni Sota," which translates to "cloudy water" or "milky water." Originally, this name described the Minnesota River, known for its slightly cloudy look caused by its clay-lined banks. Over time, this descriptive term became the name of the entire state.

Minnesota was the thirty-second state to join the Union. It officially joined on May 11, 1858.

Minnesota is located in the in the upper Midwestern region of the United States. The state shares its borders with four other states: Wisconsin to the east, Iowa to the south, and South Dakota and North Dakota to the west. Additionally, Minnesota has an international border with Canada to the north.

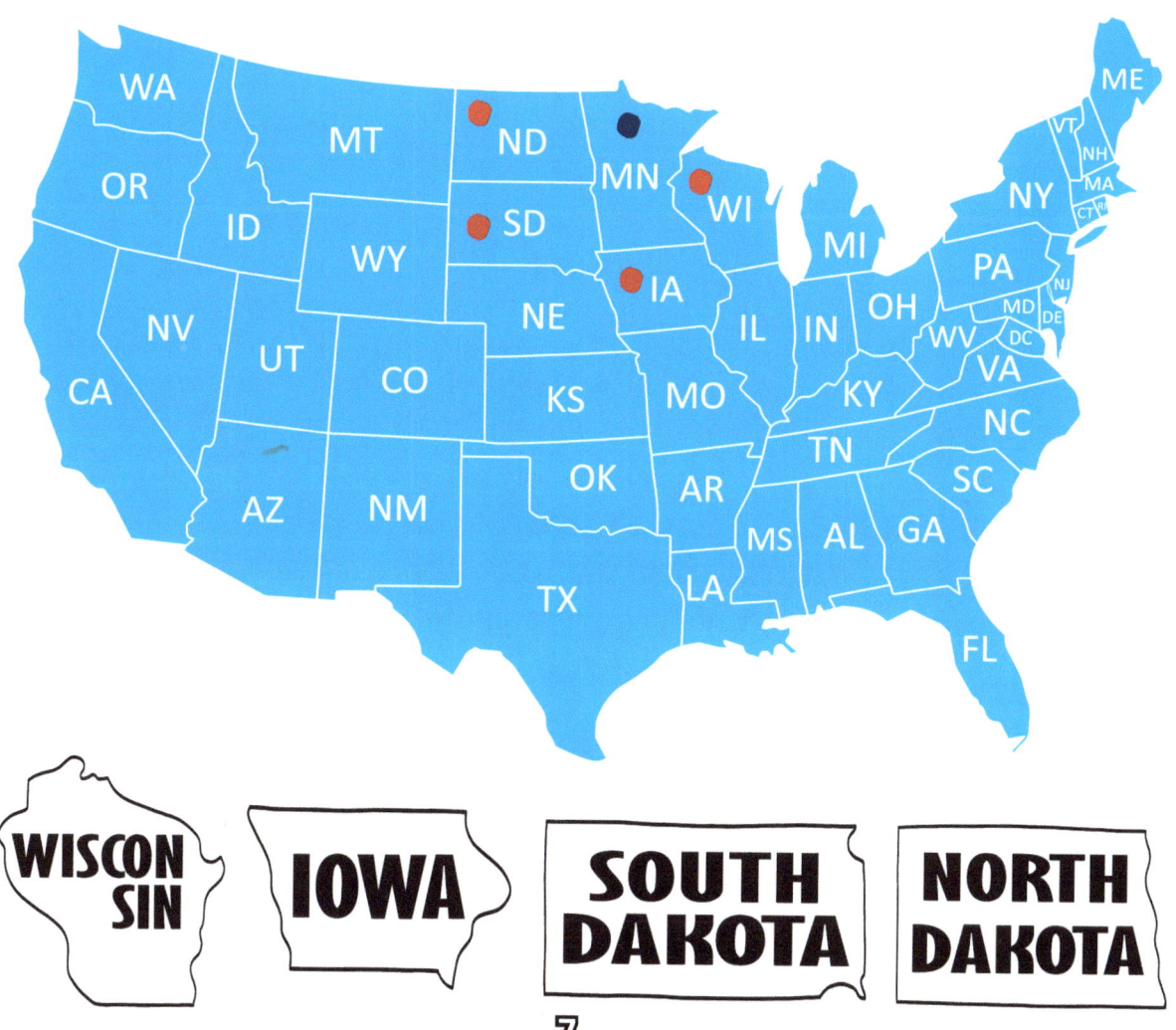

Saint Paul is the capital of Minnesota. It officially became the capital in 1849.

St. Paul, Minnesota, has an estimated population of about 303,820 people.

Minnesota State Capitol

Minnesota ranks as the twelfth largest state in the United States by area, making it one of the more significant states in the country.

F. Scott Fitzgerald was born in St. Paul, Minnesota, in 1896. He wrote the famous book The Great Gatsby and is considered one of the best writers of the 20th century.

Minnesota is home to the famous Stone Arch Bridge in Minneapolis, which was the first bridge to cross the Mississippi River.

Minnesota

There are 87 counties in Minnesota.

Here is a list of 20 of those counties:

Anoka	Dakota	Jackson	Mower
Benton	Fillmore	Kittson	Nobles
Carver	Grant	Le Sueur	Olmsted
Clay	Houston	Marshall	Ramsey
Cook	Isanti	Meeker	Wadena

The first Minnesota State Fair was held in 1859, and it's known for its fun activities, rides, and food.

The state tree of Minnesota is the Norway Pine, also known as the Red Pine.

ADVENTURE

Minnesota has over 75 state parks where you can enjoy hiking, swimming, and camping.

The state fish of Minnesota is the Walleye, a popular fish for fishing and eating in the state.

18

The state bird of Minnesota is the Common Loon (Gavia immer), commonly referred to as the Great Northern Diver. This designation was made official on March 13, 1961.

The official state flower for Minnesota is the Pink Lady's Slipper. It became the official state flower in 1902.

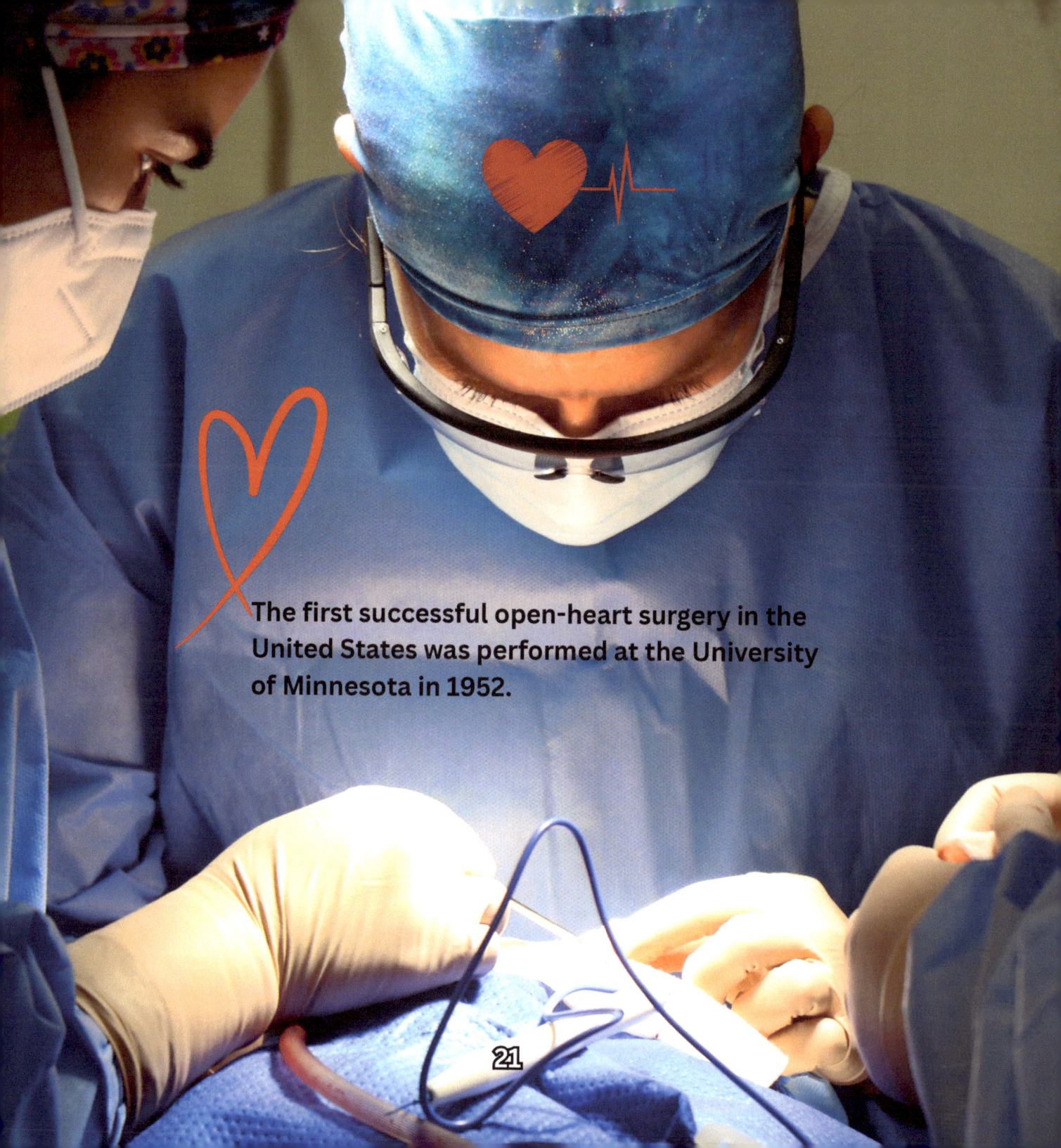

The first successful open-heart surgery in the United States was performed at the University of Minnesota in 1952.

Minnesota has some cool nicknames! It's called the "Land of 10,000 Lakes" because it has so many lakes. It's also known as the "Gopher State" because of its history with fur trading. And it's known as the "North Star State" because it's up north and follows strong values.

 STATE

  STATE

The official state motto, L'Étoile du Nord, translates to "The Star of the North" in French.

The current state flag of Minnesota was officially adopted on May 11, 2024.

Some of the crops grown in Minnesota are barley, corn, soybeans, sugar beets, and wheat.

Some of the animals that live in Minnesota include bald eagles, black bears, fox squirrels, and moose.

Minnesota experiences extreme temperatures. The highest recorded was 114 degrees Fahrenheit in Moorhead, Minnesota on July 6, 1936. The lowest was -60 degrees Fahrenheit (60 degrees below zero) in Tower on February 2, 1996.

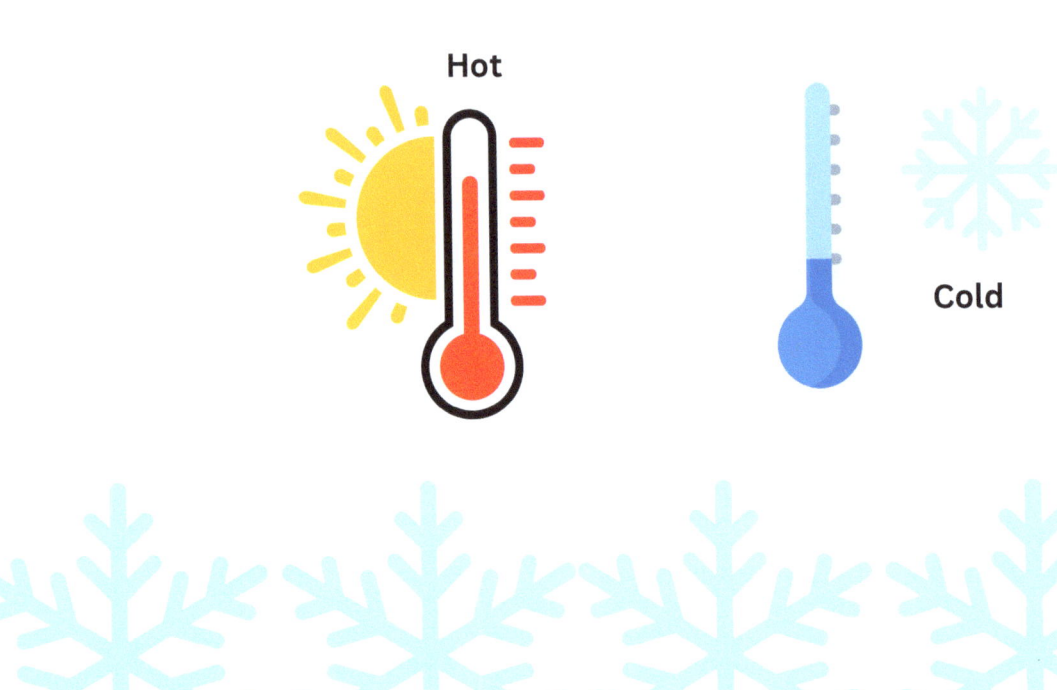

Minnesota is a major producer of wild rice, which grows in the state's lakes and wetlands.

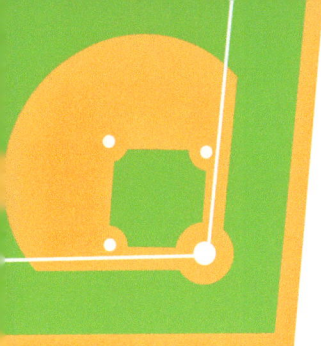   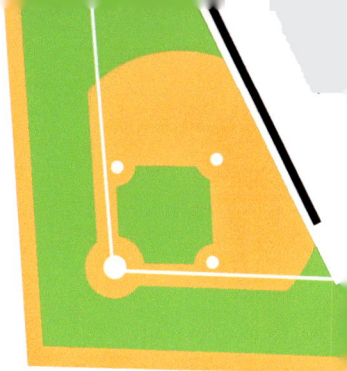

The Minnesota Twins are the state's awesome baseball team! Named after the Twin Cities, Minneapolis and Saint Paul, they play their home games at a big stadium called Target Field. The Twins have won the World Series twice, in 1987 and 1991, making their fans super proud.

31

The Minnesota Vikings are Minnesota's football team, and they play in a super cool stadium called U.S. Bank Stadium in Minneapolis. The Vikings have made it to the Super Bowl four times, showing off their strength and determination.

Lake Wobegon is a fictional town created by storyteller Garrison Keillor. It became famous through his radio show, A Prairie Home Companion. While not a real place, it reflects the charm of small-town Minnesota, with its close-knit community and unique characters. Lake Wobegon celebrates Minnesota's traditions and love of storytelling.

Scotch tape was invented in 1930 by Richard Drew, an engineer at 3M in St. Paul, Minnesota. Made from clear cellophane and adhesive, it became popular during the Great Depression for fixing everyday items. This iconic creation highlights Minnesota's history of innovation.

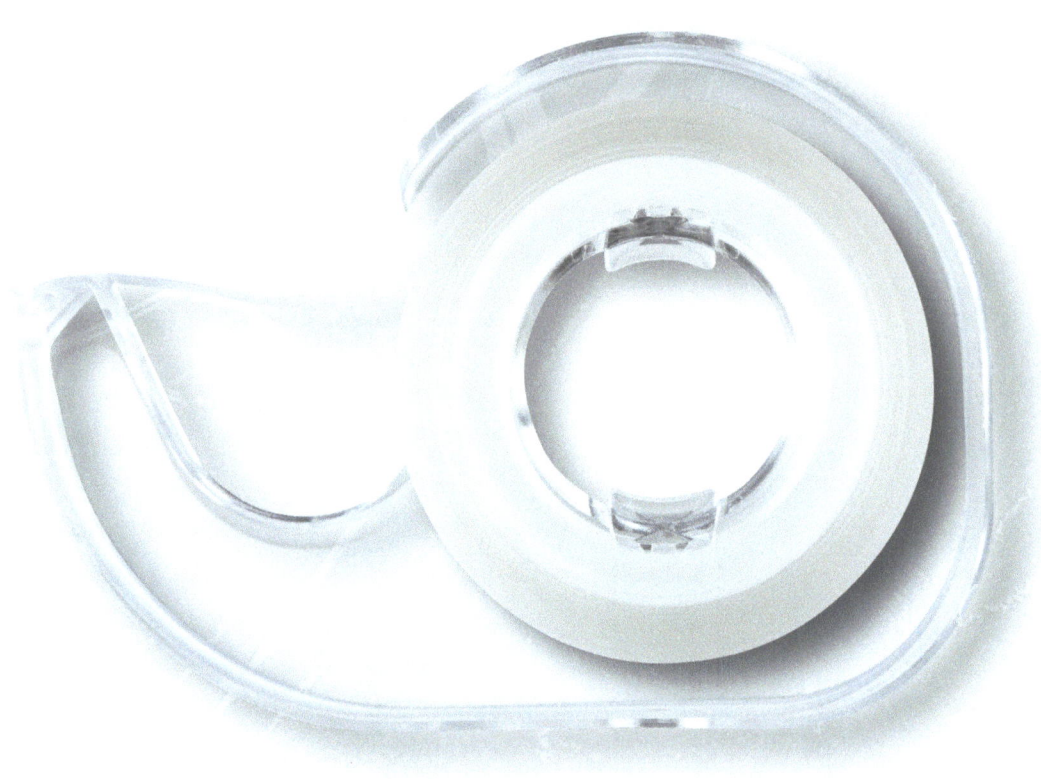

Can you name these?

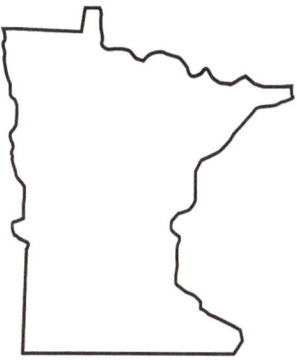

I hope you enjoyed
learning about
Minnesota.

To explore fun facts about the other 49 states, visit my website at www.joeysavestheday.com. You'll also find a wide variety of homeschool resources to support joyful learning at home. If you enjoyed this book, I would be grateful if you left a review. Your feedback truly helps. Thank you for your support!

Check out these other interesting books in the
50 States Fact Books Series!

  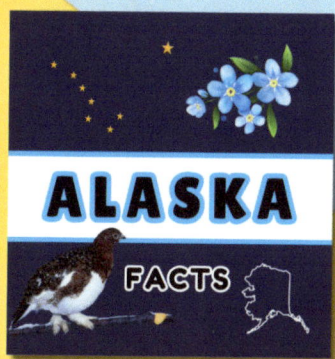

www.mimibooks.com

www.ingramcontent.com/pod-product-compliance
Lightning Source LLC
Chambersburg PA
CBHW040028050426
42453CB00002B/39